in any form, or by any
otocopying, recording, or any
tem, without permission in

L & RELIGIOUS

Company

◆ FriesenPress

One Printers Way
Altona, MB, ROG OBO
Canada

www.friesenpress.com

ISBN
978-1-03-911797-6 (Hardcover)
978-1-03-911796-9 (Paperback)
978-1-03-911798-3 (eBook)

1. POETRY, SUBJECTS & THEMES, INSPIRATION

Distributed to the trade by The Ingram Boo

Preface

A Poetry Gift is dedicated to the young and old, and those who value the good things in life. It is intended to touch the heart and soul, in a way that brings positive thoughts and happiness. Over the course of a few years, and events, I continued to write down my thoughts, which I hope will touch the hearts of many.

Table of Contents

The Thought

We remember a thought, then it's gone
It vanished in time, our dreams go on

Some are mad, some are sad
Some are happy, those thoughts we had

We talk out loud and sing a song
We write them down or hum along

You see a picture in your mind
A life some cherish and leave behind

We stop to think, and take the time
To use our gift, our special mind

We create peace and love
Glance at the sky, the stars above

It's time to rest, a busy day
Write down thoughts we could not say

It came, it went, we know a lot
Now close your eyes...and think a thought

A Bird's Eye View

A little egg up in a tree
Tucked in a nest in Tennessee

A sunny day, a chirping sound
Up in a tree above the ground

Now it's time to spread a wing
And try to fly this early spring

Away she goes up high away
A blue sky dance, a sky to play

Looking down at trees a few
A wonderful thing...

A bird's eye view

The Tree

A branch of life, I walk along
The limb of this tree, crooked and long

It's way up high, up in the sky
The bird lands and babies cry

A caterpillar crawls, on this limb
The blood of life runs within

Leaves grow, leaves fall
Reaching up high for us all

Up and down, left or right
A beautiful thing, day or night

Full of life, that looks just right
A butterfly lands, a bird takes flight

An incredible thing, for you and me
It's God's gift...

this beautiful tree

Five Kids in a Car

It's summertime, they're out of school
Going on a trip, holidays are cool

Mom and Dad, in the wagon's front seat
All the kids packed in, with jittery feet
Pushing and poking, they all complain
Sitting so close to each other again

Isn't it fun to go on a long drive?
The holiday trip and try to survive

Will Mom and Dad pull out their hair?
A beer and a cigarette might repair

Yelling and screaming, bags on the roof
"I gotta pee," "I have a sore tooth!"

They've heard it all, they're parents, you see
A poke in the eye, or a scraped knee

It takes great parents to go that far
To have control of five kids in a car

A Road

We travel on this hardened thing
We travel on and talk and sing

We go to work with friends and play
Along this road, I'd have to say

It's lonely out here late at night
We steer the road and feel alright

We think about family, we think about friends
We drive this darned road again and again

Big or small or motorbike
We drive all day, we drive all night

To get to places we must see
To visit friends or family

We grasp the wheel in driving mode
Along this path...

We call a road

A Full Bright Moon

Look at that, up in the sky
It shines so bright, we wonder why

So big and full for us to see
Above the town for you and me

A special gift so bright and round
Up in the sky it shines out proud

I feel at peace, staring above
A full bright moon...

With peace and love

Clear Twinkle Night

I know things are tough and you're full of sorrow
Just keep your chin up and try for tomorrow
With hearts sunk deep and a teary eye
We pay our respects and wonder why

Through the pain and the sorrow, a place in our dreams
We'll always remember what love really means
It's really okay, to look up at the stars
And talk to your friends, and go out in your cars

Go out of town, away from the light
And pick a spot, on a really clear night
Turn off the key, turn off the lights
Look up at the sky, on that really clear night

Now talk to your friend, or your family loved one
And tell them you care, and love them a ton
You can say a prayer to the one above
And shed some tears and swallow your love

Now dry your eyes and go on your way
Back to your loved ones I'd have to say
When you're feeling sad and not quite right
Look up at the stars...

On a clear twinkle night

A Little Blue Bird

From the time it hatched way up a tree
A miracle happened with wings you see

It flies around up in the sky
It must be amazing to learn how to fly

They look down upon us like we're all little ants
They sing and fly a blue sky dance

A shiny clean car, a windshield turd
I just got a gift...

From a little blue bird

The Orca Whale

Black and white a beautiful sight
Gliding along, a water flight

Singing and swimming, one of God's creatures
So much beauty, with black and white features

So scarce and free, swimming along
For us to see, can't go wrong

So very big, yet so very frail
A beautiful sight...

That orca whale

The Ocean Night

I walk alone on the rocky shores
The seagulls fly, the ocean roars

A large ship passes in the night
The foggy mist, the twinkle light

I crawl inside my tent again
My sleeping bag, a drop of rain

I hear the sounds, that sound just right
The sounds I love...

The ocean night

Tired Eyes

From the time we wake up, to the time we rest
The happy times, those are the best

We work, we play, we run around
We drive our cars and mess around

Day and night, we're busy bees
We run around with tired knees

At the end of the day, when we finally lay down
We take a deep breath, a smile or a frown

We wash our face, climb into bed
Sore feet, sore eyes, a very sore head

A last deep breath with darkened skies
We finally close...

Our tired eyes

A Wish

Our hopes and dreams, it's who we are
We walk, we run, we drive our car

Most of us live, work and play
Keeping things in our own way

To stop the bad or make some good
We make a wish, a wish that could

A wishing well or in the sky
A birthday cake, a teary eye

Treat wishes well, don't treat them bad
Someone's listening, to the wish we had

So throw in that coin, or a birthday cake
Our hopes and dreams...

A wish we make

That Turkey

Fall is here, it's cold outside
Turkeys run and try to hide

Thanksgiving Day, family and friends
A great big meal, they all attend

To be together and enjoy that bird
And to give thanks, a speech is heard

The house smells great, everyone's here
The table's set, it's getting near

Everyone sits with a knife and fork
To eat that bird, a turkey dork

But it's a special day, do you know why?
Because of that turkey...

And pumpkin pie

Truck Driving Man

Shifting gears, reflectors shine
Midnight rain, the road is mine

Pouring rain, a windshield dance
Dotted lines, a stare, a glance

Headed home, on the phone
Headset rings, kids alone

Climbing up, I see the moon
I'm shifting gears, I'll be there soon

I stop and look up at the sky
And say a prayer, and then I sigh

I climb back in the driver's seat
My Kenworth sings, it's new and neat

I'm finally home, coming down the hill
To park my rig, head home I will

I work so hard, I know I can
My kids, my life...

Truck driving man

A Christmas Wish

Seasons come and seasons go
Leaves will fall and wind will blow

The air is getting cold and crisp
Winter's here, a Christmas list

The holiday's full of Christmas cheer
Family, friends, and loved ones near

A turkey dinner, a pie or two
A Christmas wish...

From me to you

I love the Snow

Falling down, white and fresh
See the snow, feel the best

With a friend, it's so cool
Making breakfast, a coffee rule

Winter's here, music's on
The cabin's great, summer's gone

Take a break, a firewood day
The snow is falling, it feels okay

A snowflake flight, a winter sight
A white blanket, I feel alright

That time of year, I reckon so
The air is crisp...

I love the snow

For the love of God

Stay clean and safe, for the love of God
Please follow the rules, for the love of God

Protect your family, for the love of God
Through sickness and health, for the love of God
We can get through this, for the love of God
If you're sick, isolate, for the love of God

Read a book, or write a letter, for the love of God
Our health workers, our heroes, for the love of God

Stick together while we're apart, for the love of God
Believe in yourself and others, for the love of God

And if you ask sincerely for the love of God
Your prayers might be answered

If you ask...

For the love of God

The Crow

Hungry eyes, a cold stare
Destination, a cloud to spare

A black-bird bellows, a morning song
A piercing sound, right or wrong

Another poem I have to write
My thoughts are here, a beautiful sight

Free as a bird, a black bird sings
Cold hard stare, a feathered wing

A breezy day, the wind will blow
An innocent stare...

The bird, the crow.

The Grass

Out in the yard, I work and clean
My yard is nice, the grass is green

My kids run, my kids play
They laugh and yell, I have to say

My dogs run, my dogs play
They bark and jump, and have their way

Kids and dogs, they have a blast
I just stepped on a turd in the grass

Make it Rain

It's been a long hot one, there's no clouds in sight
The planes are flying, the people are crying
It's been one heck of a fight
Some people say you have to pray, to help heal the pain
If there's anyone up there listening,
Come on please make it rain
Oh Lord now make it rain, and help stop all these flames
Please put a cloud over top of me and help stop all this pain
Some people say you have to pray, to help heal the pain
If there's anyone up there listening,
Come on please make it rain
B.C.'s on fire and people are tired, it's such a gruesome sight
That mother nature lashed out at us,
It burned all day and night
Please put a cloud over top of me and help stop all this pain
If there's anyone up there listening,
Come on please make it rain
Now I have to say in my own way, please stop all this pain
We need to kneel, we need to prey
Oh Lord please make it rain

Go to Sleep

Sometimes I lay down in my bed
And stare at the ceiling, thoughts in my head

Of the day gone by and the things I've seen
I close my eyes and try to dream

I think about family, I think about friends
Night after night, again and again

Did I do the things I wanted to do?
I lay and wonder a thing or two

It's time to rest and get some sleep
I pray to God, my soul to keep

I hear the wind, it's cold outside
I'm in my mind, that's where I'll hide

I'm finally at rest, my thoughts are deep
A final deep breath...

Now go to sleep.

The Butterfly

I crawl along on my world this tree
I'm just a little caterpillar you see

It's been a while, it's time to rest
In my cocoon, it's dark at best

When the time is right and it's warm outside
I'll emerge at last and go and hide

I'll wait and grow and look around
At my new world up off the ground

When the time is right, I'll fly away
It could be April or maybe May

The children laugh and run and play
And try to catch me. "No way!" I say

I'll find some friends to fly with me
A bunch of us for you to see

I'll fly up high
Into the sky
I'm wild and free
I'm a butterfly

The Guitar

Made of wood, if I could
If I should write a song

Strum a tune, happy thought
Dream a dream, sing along

Pick a cord, play a tune
Happy life, full bright moon

Pick it up, build a song
Was I right, was I wrong?

Take flight like a bird
For the song that I heard

Take a break, branch to take
Tree of life by a lake

A deep breath, a music ride
Keep going, don't hide

Made of wood, if I could
If I should, write a song...

The guitar

Put On Your Favourite Song

Sometimes life can be stressful and long,
Without the joy of a really good song

It makes us smile when times are rough,
It makes us sing when times are tough

It may be the flames that affect all of us,
It may be the poor kids on a hockey team bus

We can't help the sorrow and the feelings inside,
When times are tough we want to sleep and hide

It might be family or maybe a friend,
That passes away suddenly, and we're all sad again
But down that road and in our hearts,
We heal and keep going, we can't fall apart

So remember when you need to heal all the pain
Put on your favourite song and feel happy again

The Snow Bird

Flying high
Into the sky
A wonderful sight
As they take flight

Proud and strong
In times of need
They fly up high
With precision speed

Thoughts and prayers
A sudden thing
The tears will fall
Our hearts will sing

A prayer, a thought, a spoken word

At heaven's gate...

The snow bird.

To Heal Our Heart

We're still here every night
Working hard, a highway flight

From then 'til now, we drive along
The tires sing a nightly song

Nuts and bolts inside my back
I wished I owned a Cadillac

Our kids at home, spirits high
lean ahead, look at the sky

I write my words and write my song
While you sleep I drive along

A laugh, a cry, a smile, a grin
Don't look down, keep up your chin

We've been through the toughest part...

Now I write to heal our heart

Should I

Should we do
Should we try
Should we laugh
Should we cry

Gather up
Staying strong
Even when things go wrong

Think of friends
Think of life
Happy thoughts
Happy wife

Take a breath
Close your eyes
Reset thoughts, wonder why

Change your way, here to stay
Always Dad, kids to play

Have to say, have to do
Kids depend, it's on you

Be proud, an open eye
Never say...

Should I

Peanut Butter and Jelly

Sometimes life can get you down
And you need a pick me up

Get out the knife
Get out the bread
Hold it steady, and get ready
For peanut butter and jelly

Life can be tough, and life can be busy
Sometimes life can make us dizzy

Get out the knife
Get out the bread
Hold it steady, and get ready
For peanut butter and jelly

Remember When

A day to think, a day to pray
The sun will shine, a special day

They served their country, a golden heart
A soldier's dream, they stand apart

A fallen hero at heaven's gate
A salute to them, don't hesitate

To say a prayer up in the sky
A thought out loud, a teary eye

A poppy field, a day for them
A thought, a prayer...

Remember when

November Rain

Summer's past, it went so fast
The air is crisp and clean

The trees are bare, it's cold out there
The leaves have lost their green

Halloween fun, October's done
Get out the hockey gear
It's eight degrees, I'm raking leaves
December's almost here

Remembrance Day has come and past
A poppy flower to gain
A water drop fell from the clouds
I love November rain

Winter

The summer's gone, the cold is near
The leaves drift down, the sky is clear
No more bikes for kids to ride
All our pets will hide inside

One cold morning we'll see the snow
The kids will laugh and run, you know
They'll grab their coats, boots, and gloves
And run outside with clouds above

They'll zoom down hills on top their sleds
Scream and yell and bonk their heads
We'll drive our cars and slip and slide
Strap on some skis, down hill we'll glide

Then one day we'll dance with glee
It's Christmas time, let's get a tree
A beautiful time of year to see
Kids and friends and family

The world's a beautiful thing you know
Cold and crisp and covered in snow
The snow will fall, the wind will blow
So bundle up...

It's winter you know

Summer Rain

A rainy May, a summer day
A moistened leaf, a cloud to stay

A moistened branch, a shiny wing
A bird's quick flight, to fly and sing

A child plays, a puddle dance
Rubber boots, umbrella prance

A lovely sight for us to gain
The sky is crying...

With summer rain

The Guitar on the Chair

When I'm driving along, humming a song
Steering at night, feeling alright

It's a beautiful thing, an earful ring
It's lonely out there, the guitar on the chair

They're both made of wood, stand proud like they should
A craftsmanship's work, life's little perk

When I get home, I can't wait to strum
A word to write, a song to hum

It's a beautiful thing, an earful ring
It's lonely out there...

The guitar on the chair

love to Fly

Brand new wings, wait to arrive
Poke through the dark shell sky

Heal the pain, fly high
Feel free, beautiful sky

The air above the flying dove
Blackbirds sing, wings of love

A seagull flies above the sea
The waves crash on you and me
A beach, a mountain, a tree, a sky
Free birds sing...

And love to fly

The Kite

From the package, a kid, a smile
Put it together in a while

Plastic and parts, a string I see
Let's go outside, it's so windy

I threw it up, it flew with ease
Hang on strong, a kite trapeze

It's free, it flies up high to see
A kid, a smile for you and me

When life is hard and you need a break
Grab your kite, time to take

Big or small, the windy flight
A breezy day, the sky...

The kite

That Life

From the time we arrive and open our eyes
We laugh and play and sometimes cry
We grow and grow, we're happy, we're mad
We learn about things from our mom and dad

We meet someone and have kids of our own
Now they run and play, the playground zone

We all grow old and get on in age
Our hair turns white like silver sage

Eventually it's our children's turn
To live their life, to work and earn

I'll never forget the good times I had
With my kids and family, I'm so glad

It may be a child, it may be a pet
A walk in the rain, we're all getting wet

Whatever it is, a husband or wife
We're only here once...

So please cherish that life

Goodbye

We met one day, way back when
From that day on, you were my friend

Now I have to say goodbye
You're in my thoughts as days go by

I'll always find the time to think
About my friend, a smile, a wink

When I cry or have a frown
I take a breath and write it down

The stars above, the starlit sky
I close my eyes...

And say goodbye

My Black Cat

She looks at me with innocent eyes
A purr, a meow, winter skies

Waiting for food or a scratch on the head
Sleeping on the foot of my king-size bed

Always my friend through thick and thin
At my feet, love within

It's nice to have a little friend
In the window waiting again

Waiting for food on her little mat
A great little friend... my black cat.

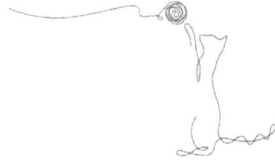

love

It starts with a smile, or maybe a wink
A good gesture, a feeling I think

A feeling inside, a lonely heart
Or maybe a treat, a raspberry tart

An automobile, or maybe a bike
A walk on a path, or flying a kite

It could be a friend, or maybe a pet
Or a rainy day, a dance getting wet

An ice-cream cone, a lemon-filled pie
A beautiful sparkle, in someone's eye

A beautiful night, the stars will shine
A thought, a prayer, a glass of wine

It could be a hug, or maybe a kiss
Waving goodbye, to someone you'll miss

All these things that capture our heart
A wonderful feeling that sets them apart

Nothing compares or rises above
The best of the best...

The things that we love.

Into the Dark

I close my eyes, I take a break
Fade to black, investigate

The sun goes down, the moon comes out
The stars will shine, coyotes shout

The day is done, I go to sleep
I rest my aching throbbing feet

An owl's hoot, a cat's meow
I close my thoughts, and dream somehow

It all slows down, a dream to start
I drift away...

Into the dark.

It's What I Miss

Sea to sea, east to west, the people are in trouble
It's come to this, a scary thing, to live inside a bubble
It doesn't matter how old you are, race or skin colour
We're all in this together my friends, the earth is called our mother
You could be poor, you could be rich, cook a meal or sew a stitch
You fix a car, or paint a house, an elephant or just a mouse
In a town or country, you're black or white, it's you, it's me
Something inside, it's always there. A feeling, a thought, a smile,
a stare
Please put aside your guilt and greed
Dig a hole and plant a seed
From sea to sea, I know its worth. Our precious soil, our planet Earth
A prayer, a nod, a hand to shake. A boat, a fish upon a lake
To fly up high or walk along
We have to pray and get along
To lie and cheat or arrogance
Will never work, it works against
Life is so special for you and me
Our kids all play under a tree
Please don't fight or hesitate
To lend a hand, it's in our fate
The soil we use, the air we breathe
A life we live, roll up your sleeve
Telephone or internet, it really doesn't matter
Keep in touch and be kind, all that Facebook chatter
So now's our chance to realize, life's little bumps, we hide inside
The Earth, the sky, a hug, a kiss
Can't we be friends? It's what I miss.

The Busy Beaver

Building building here we go
Rushing down water flow

Sticks and branches swim along
Canadian beaver proud and strong

Building its home the way they do
To raise their babies one or two

When it's done it's cool inside
Under the water they swim and hide

It's proud and strong, a great achiever
A hideaway home, that busy beaver

The Farm

The food that we eat and the tractor seat
The corn they know, the wheat they grow
They're a special breed with all the feed
A chicken and a cow, a horse and a plow

An orchard field, an orange peeled
A rubber boot, pull up a root
What would we do without some stew
With carrots and potatoes, for me and you

A wonderful thing along with a barn
From dawn till dusk...

They work on the farm

The Cat and the Mouse

There once was a cat, who hunted a mouse
Sneaking around a great big house
One day he found one and was ready to pounce
When all of a sudden, the mouse stood up to announce

Hold on one minute you crazy cat
Let me explain this and that
Let's hangout and jump and play
And have some fun and sleep all day

You share your food, I'll share my cheese
Let's not fight oh please oh please
From that day on in that big house
They were best friends...

The cat and the mouse

The Ferris Wheel

Up high in the sky, a wonderful sight
A nervous feeling, hang on tight

Climb in the big chair, to go up in the air
Hit the top and see, people like you and me

I love to look out over the hills
The special feeling and all the thrills

On top of the world, a world of joy
The carnival's here, a smile to deploy

A couple dollars to ride along
To go up high and sing a song

A bird's eye view, it's quite unreal
To ride up high...

On the Ferris wheel

The Campfire

Life is so busy, we can't slow down
To take a break, from a city or town

A flickering light, a beautiful sight
To relax and stare, to an ember in there

Different shapes, an orange glow
Moving and dancing, imagination show

Sitting there in our chair, our kids with a marshmallow stick
They eat the whole bag, a sticky mess, a marshmallow finger
to lick

A relaxing retreat, a lawn chair seat, I can't wait to retire
To sit and relax from this high-pace world, a chair by the
orange campfire

Time Flies

Day after day, night after night
We work, we play, and feel alright

We get up every morning, we're busy bees
With worn-out hands, and achy knees

We fix our cars, and build a house
As big as an elephant, or small as a mouse

We look at the clock, or the sunset
The weeks go by, the older we get

The year's tick on, the lows and the highs
We realize then...

How time flies

The Workaholic

We work all day, we work all night
We work our fingers to the bone

Fixing a car, or making some food
Some jobs take us from home

To make some money, and a career
I need a day off, is the weekend near?

A train conductor, or a truck driver
A painter, or a deep-sea diver

The ships will sail, the planes will fly
We work so hard and wonder why

Raising our kids to jump and frolic
I need a day off...

I'm a workaholic

A Quiet Sound

Early in the morning or late at night
Out in a tent or on a flight

We hear the sounds that fill our ears
The buzzing sound, a fly appears

A dove singing on a high wire
The highway sound of a semi tire

The growling sound of a hunger pain
I hear the sound of a bird again

The embarrassing sound of a cheek on a bench
A hammer on a thumb, the pain and the clench

When it all slows down, all around
It's usually a good time...

For a quiet sound

Imagination

It may be a dream late at night
It may be a book that just feels right

An image in a child's eye, riding on the wings of a bird in
the sky
A movie or story that we all like, landing on the moon, or flying
a kite

Space travel or an army of ants
A marching band or a ballet dance

The thoughts and images in our head
A planet of green, or a planet of red

Things that keep us going, like a train in a station
A wonderful thing...

Our imagination

Open the Door

A broken heart or things within
A stubborn mind, or next of kin

A friend in need is a friend indeed
Let's build a garden and plant a seed

Sometimes we need time alone
To think about things, to think about home

Someone to talk to, a holding hand
To help us heal, or help us stand

Just always remember, I'm always there
A teary eye, a lonely stare

I'll give you my hand if you need more
Just come on in...

I'll open the door

Tick-Tock

As time goes on and minutes roll by
The sun will rise up in the sky
A minute, an hour, or maybe a day
Hustle and bustle, we work, we play

Monday comes, and Monday goes
Tuesday, Wednesday, Thursday flows
Can't wait for Friday, the weekend's here
Let's have some fun and get in gear

Days and nights, weeks roll by
Our hair turns grey, we wonder why
The years roll by, a funny thing
Time flies on, a beautiful wing

We work, we sing, we dance, we walk
Time will tell
Tick-Tock, Tick-Tock

The Lost Soul

On this day, we have to pray, kneel and close our eyes
The children there, an innocent stare
So many years gone by

To drift along, and not be found, a raft out in the sea
A lonely hand, a teary eye
To miss your family

A hopeful day, a time to pray, we shine a bright spotlight
With saddened hearts, and holding hands
It shines so very bright

You've found the path, and make your way, to the
shining light
A helpful hand, a spoken word, to finally make it right

To rest in peace at heaven's gate, a little child's face
We guide you home, you're not alone...

you're in a sacred place

F. A. PELLE